ANIMAL POEMS

illustrated by
MEG RUTHERFORD

Selected by Polly Richardson

BARRON'S

First edition for the United States and Canada published 1992
by Barron's Educational Series, Inc.

First published in Great Britain in 1992 by Simon & Schuster Young
Books, Campus 400, Maylands Avenue, Hemel Hempstead HP2 7EZ.

Illustrations copyright © 1992 Meg Rutherford

All inquiries should be addressed to:
Barron's Educational Series, Inc.
250 Wireless Boulevard
Hauppauge, New York 11788

Library of Congress Catalog Card No. 92-2784

International Standard Book No. 0-8120-6283-3

Library of Congress Cataloging-in-Publication Data

Animal poems / illustrated by Meg Rutherford : selected by Polly
    Richardson. – 1st ed. for the U.S. and Canada.
        p.   cm.
    Summary: An illustrated collection of poems by a variety of
American and English authors.
    ISBN 0-8120-6283-3
    1. Animals—Juvenile poetry. 2. Children's poetry, American.
3. Children's poetry, English. [1. Animals—Poetry. 2. American
poetry—Collections. 3. English poetry—Collections.]
I. Rutherford, Meg. ill.   II. Richardson, Polly.
PS595.A5A53   1992
811.008′036—dc20   92-2784
                                                          CIP
                                                          AC

PRINTED IN BELGIUM
2345 987654321

Contents

Mr. Tigeroo

Excuse me, Mr. Tigeroo
Please tell me what's come over you.
You used to be a jungle cat
Who'd prowl and stalk and rarely chat.
But now you smile and wag your tail
And file sharp points on every nail.
You brush your teeth, you comb your hair
I hear you've even swept your lair.
Don't try to fool *me*, Tigeroo
I won't become a meal for you!

Joe Friedman

Mice

I think mice
Are rather nice.
Their tails are long,
Their faces small,
They haven't any
Chins at all.
Their ears are pink,
Their teeth are white,
They run about
The house at night.
They nibble things
They shouldn't touch
And no one seems
To like them much.

But *I* think mice
Are nice.

Rose Fyleman

Barney and Fred

Fancy eating your bed
Like the guinea pigs Barney and Fred
Who nibble away
Wood shavings and hay.

I would never feel
Like making my house a meal
And gnawing the wood
To do my teeth good.

I never met anyone yet
Who ate the floor and carpet
Except, as I said,
Barney and Fred.

Stanley Cook

A Little Talk

The big brown hen and Mrs. Duck
Went walking out together.
They talked about all sorts of things—
The farmyard, and the weather.
But all *I* heard was "Cluck!
    Cluck! Cluck!"
And "Quack! Quack! Quack!"
    from Mrs. Duck.

Anon

The Snail

Snail upon the wall,
Have you got at all
Anything to tell
about your shell?

Only this, my child—
when the wind is wild,
Or when the sun is hot,
it's all I've got.

John Drinkwater

The Mole

The Mole for breakfast likes to munch
A dozen worms, the same for lunch.
For tea and supper—can you guess?
More worms, you say? The answer's yes.
In fact, the humble Mole can do
What is impossible for you.
(Unless you are prepared to say
You could eat sixty worms a day?)

Dick King-Smith

Bees

Every bee
that
ever was
was
partly
sting
and partly
. . . buzz.

Jack Prelutsky

7

In the Bush

In the bush
you might see
koalas dozing in a tree.
In the bush
you might hear
kangaroos thumping
very near,
lizards scuttling
through dry grass,
noisy parrots
flying past.
In the bush
tread with care—
you never know
what's hiding there!

Anne Le Roy

Kangaroos

Kangaroos are hoppity
Kangaroos are fun.
If you want to catch a Kangaroo
You'll really have to run!

Kangaroos are jumpy
Bounding over the plain,
You can't hold down a Kangaroo
'Cause he'll bounce up again.

Kangaroos are tough guys
They can box as well.
If a Kangaroo should hit you
Your head rings like a bell!

Kangaroo moms are kindly
For their young they have a pocket,
Where babes can feed and feel quite safe
While Mom takes off like a rocket!

John Cotton

Five Little Owls

Five little owls in an old elm tree,
Fluffy and puffy as owls could be,
Blinking and winking with big round eyes
At the big round moon that hung in the skies.
As I passed beneath, I could hear one say,
"There'll be mouse for supper, there will, today!"
Then all of them hooted "Tu-whit, Tu-whoo!
Yes, mouse for supper, Hoo hoo, Hoo hoo!"

Anon

The Cow

The friendly cow, all red and white,
I love with all my heart.
She gives me cream with all her might,
To eat with apple tart.

She wanders lowing here and there,
And yet she cannot stray,
All in the pleasant open air,
The pleasant light of day.

And blown by all the winds that pass,
And wet with all the showers,
She walks among the meadow grass
And eats the meadow flowers.

Robert Louis Stevenson

Brock the Badger

Brock the Badger.
Shy, gruff.
Coat rough,
White, black, gray.
Sleeps all day.
Dear Brock.

Brock the Badger.
Walks at night
Till light.
Shhh! – beware!
Who's there?
It's dear Brock.

Dennis Hamley

12

Alligator

If you want to see an alligator
you must go down to the muddy slushy end
of the old Caroony River.

I know an alligator
who's living down there
She's a-big. She's a-mean. She's a-wild.
She's a-fierce.

But if you really want to see an alligator
you must go down to the muddy slushy end
of the old Caroony River.

Go down gently to that river and say
"Alligator Mama
Alligator Mama
Alligator Mamaaaaaaaa"

And up she'll rise
but don't stick around
RUN FOR YOUR LIFE!

Grace Nichols

Whisky Frisky

Whisky Frisky, hippity-hop
Up he goes to the treetop!

Whirly, twirly, round and round,
Down he scampers to the ground.

Furly, curly, what a tail!
Tall as a feather, broad as a sail!

Where's his supper? In the shell.
Snappity, crackity, out it fell.

Anon

Little Horace Rabbit

While lying very quietly,
a paw upon his nose,
Little Horace Rabbit
soon began to doze.
And as he drifted off to sleep
his mind began to think
"Wouldn't it be funny
if all my fur turned pink!"
"I hardly think that's comical,"
his conscience made a frown—
"Hog hair sometimes starts as pink,
but hare hair must be brown!"

Joe Friedman

Pussy Pussy Puddle Cat

Pussy pussy puddle cat
what do you think
you're playing at
making puddles
on the mat
chairs and tables
don't do that!

Roger McGough

16

Seal Lullaby

Oh, hush thee, my baby, the night is behind us,
And black are the waters that sparkled so green.
The moon o'er the combers, looks downward to find us
At rest in the hollows that rustle between.
Where billow meets billow, there soft be thy pillow.
Ah, weary wee flipperling, curl at thy ease!
The storm shall not wake thee, nor sharks overtake thee,
Asleep in the arms of the slow swinging sea.

Rudyard Kipling

Geraldine Giraffe

The
longest
ever
woolly
scarf
was
worn
by
Geraldine
Giraffe.
Around
her
neck
the
scarf
she
wound,
but
still
it
trailed
upon
the
ground.

Colin West

Grizzly Bear

If you ever, ever, ever meet a grizzly bear,
You must never, never, never ask him *where*
He is going.
Or *what* he is doing.
For if you ever, ever, dare
to stop a grizzly bear,
You will never meet *another* grizzly bear.

Mary Austin

19

A Memory

This I remember,
I saw from a train—
A shaggy wild pony
That stood in the rain.

Where I was going,
And where was the train,
I cannot remember,
I cannot explain.

All these years after
It comes back again—
A shaggy wild pony
That stood in the rain.

Douglas Gibson

Sunning

Old Dog lay in the summer sun
Much too lazy to rise and run.
He flapped an ear
At a buzzing fly.
He winked a half-opened
Sleepy eye.
He scratched himself
On an itching spot.
As he dozed on the porch
When the sun was hot.
He whimpered a bit
From force of habit,
While he lazily dreamed
Of chasing a rabbit.
But Old Dog happily lay in the sun,
Much too lazy to rise and run.

James S. Tippett

Three Little Puffins

Three little puffins
Were partial to muffins,
As partial as partial can be.
    They wouldn't eat nuffin
    But hot buttered muffin
For breakfast and dinner and tea.

Pantin' and puffin'
And chewin' and chuffin'
They just went on stuffin', dear me!
    Till the three little puffins
    Were chockful of muffins
And puffy as puffy can be.
                   All three
Were puffy as puffy can be.

Eleanor Farjeon

22

Spring Song

On the grassy banks
Lambkins at their pranks.
Woolly sisters, woolly brothers,
Jumping off their feet,
While their woolly mothers
Watch by them and bleat.

Christina Rossetti

A Kitten

He's nothing much but fur
And two round eyes of blue.
He has a giant purr
And a midget mew.

He darts and pats the air,
He starts and pricks his ear,
When there is nothing there
For him to see and hear.

He runs around in rings,
But why we cannot tell.
With sideways leaps he springs
At things invisible –

Then halfway through a leap
His startled eyeballs close,
And he drops off to sleep
With one paw on his nose.

Eleanor Farjeon

Bears

Bears
have few cares
When the wind blows cold and the
    snow drifts deep
they sleep and sleep and sleep and
                    sleep.

Elizabeth Coatsworth

ACKNOWLEDGEMENTS

The editor and publishers are grateful to the copyright holders for permission to use the following poems:

'Grizzly Bear' by **Mary Austin** from *Children Sing in the Far West* by Mary Austin, © 1928 by Mary Austin, copyright renewed 1956 by Kenneth M Chapman and Mary C Wheelwright, reprinted by permission of Houghton Mifflin Co. All rights reserved. 'Barney and Fred' by **Stanley Cook** from *Come Along* published by the author © the author's Estate. 'Kangaroos' by **John Cotton** by kind permission of the author. 'The Snail' by **John Drinkwater** reprinted by permission of Samuel French Ltd on behalf of the John Drinkwater Estate. 'A Kitten' by **Eleanor Farjeon** from *Invitation to A Mouse* published by Michael Joseph Ltd. 'Three Little Puffins' by **Eleanor Farjeon** from *Silver Curlew* published by Oxford University Press. 'Mr Tigeroo' and 'Little Horace Rabbit' by **Joe Friedman** copyright © 1992 by Barron's Educational Series, Inc. 'Mice' by **Rose Fyleman** by permission of The Society of Authors as the literary representative of the Estate of Rose Fyleman. 'Brock the Badger' by **Dennis Hamley** by kind permission of the author. 'The Mole' by **Dick King-Smith** by kind permission of the author. 'In the Bush' by **Anne Le Roy** from *Big Dipper* published by OUP Melbourne. 'Pussy Pussy Puddle Cat' by **Roger McGough** from *Sky in the Pie* reproduced with permission of the Peters Fraser & Dunlop Group Ltd. 'Alligator' by **Grace Nichols** reproduced with permission of Curtis Brown Group Ltd, on behalf of Grace Nichols © Grace Nichols 1984. 'Bees' by **Jack Prelutsky** from *Zoo Doings* © 1983 by Jack Prelutsky by permission of Greenwillow Books, a division of William Morrow & Co Inc. 'Daniel's Rabbit' by **Fred Sedgwick** by kind permission of the author. 'Sunning' by **James S. Tippett** from *Crickety Cricket!* by James Tippert © 1933, renewed 1973 by Martha K Tippett, reprinted by permission of Harper Collins Publishers. 'Geraldine Giraffe' by **Colin West** from *The Best of West* reprinted by permission of Hutchinson Children's Books.